# CREATIVE ARITHMI

Mathematics should be creative. Mathematics should be explorative. Mathematics should not seem like rote memory work or drudge work.

This LIFEPAC is designed to stimulate and challenge your mind. You will have an opportunity to test and refresh your basic

mathematica
chance to pu
to know tha. ... ... ...
brain that is capable of extraordinary feats. So put your brain in gear and use that wonderful potential God bestowed on you!

## OBJECTIVES

**Read these objectives.** The objectives tell you what you will be able to do when you have successfully completed this LIFEPAC.

When you have finished this LIFEPAC, you should be able

1. To add whole numbers.

2. To subtract whole numbers.

3. To multiply whole numbers.

4. To divide whole numbers.

5. To solve mathematical puzzles.

6. To name the factors of whole numbers.

7. To identify prime numbers.

8. To use creatively the basic skills of addition, subtraction, multiplication, and division.

**Survey the LIFEPAC.** Ask yourself some questions about this study. Write your questions here.

_____

_____

_____

_____

_____

_____

_____

_____

# I. BASIC ARITHMETIC SKILLS

**OBJECTIVES**

1. To add whole numbers.
2. To subtract whole numbers.
3. To multiply whole numbers.
4. To divide whole numbers.

This section of the LIFEPAC will test your basic arithmetic skills. You may know how to work all the problems already, and you may finish this section very rapidly. However, this inventory of your basic skills will also point up any areas in which you need practice. Your work in this section will refresh your skills and prepare you for the creative exercises in the following sections. As a famous philosopher once said: mathematics is the science of doing necessary things in the easiest way!

## ADDITION

Addition is the most basic arithmetic skill. Subtraction, multiplication, and division all depend on addition. You may need to review the basic addition facts before you proceed to the problems in this section.

The following figure (Figure 1) is a table of the basic addition facts. To read the table, choose a number in the top row that you wish to add. Choose another number in the left-hand column that you wish to add to the first number. To add the numbers, follow the two columns to their intersection. The intersection shows the answer for adding the two numbers together.

| +  | 0  | 1  | 2  | 3  | 4  | 5  | 6  | 7  | 8  | 9  |
|----|----|----|----|----|----|----|----|----|----|----|
| 0  | 0  | 1  | 2  | 3  | 4  | 5  | 6  | 7  | 8  | 9  |
| 1  | 1  | 2  | 3  | 4  | 5  | 6  | 7  | 8  | 9  | 10 |
| 2  | 2  | 3  | 4  | 5  | 6  | 7  | 8  | 9  | 10 | 11 |
| 3  | 3  | 4  | 5  | 6  | 7  | 8  | 9  | 10 | 11 | 12 |
| 4  | 4  | 5  | 6  | 7  | 8  | 9  | 10 | 11 | 12 | 13 |
| 5  | 5  | 6  | 7  | 8  | 9  | 10 | 11 | 12 | 13 | 14 |
| 6  | 6  | 7  | 8  | 9  | 10 | 11 | 12 | 13 | 14 | 15 |
| 7  | 7  | 8  | 9  | 10 | 11 | 12 | 13 | 14 | 15 | 16 |
| 8  | 8  | 9  | 10 | 11 | 12 | 13 | 14 | 15 | 16 | 17 |
| 9  | 9  | 10 | 11 | 12 | 13 | 14 | 15 | 16 | 17 | 18 |

Figure 1

After you have reviewed or studied the basic facts, work on the following scrambled chart. Record the time you start and finish to determine how long you take to complete the chart.

Complete this basic addition chart.

1.1

| +  | 5 | 2 | 1 | 7 | 6 | 3 | 4 | 8 | 9 |
|----|---|---|---|---|---|---|---|---|---|
| 7  |   |   |   |   |   |   |   |   |   |
| 3  |   |   |   |   |   |   |   |   |   |
| 8  |   |   |   |   |   |   |   |   |   |
| 2  |   |   |   |   |   |   |   |   |   |
| 9  |   |   |   |   |   |   |   |   |   |
| 1  |   |   |   |   |   |   |   |   |   |
| 4  |   |   |   |   |   |   |   |   |   |
| 5  |   |   |   |   |   |   |   |   |   |
| 6  |   |   |   |   |   |   |   |   |   |

Time:   minutes _____

seconds _____

Number missed _____

Review each of the addition facts that you missed. For extra practice you may make your own scrambled fact chart. Try to get your completion time under two minutes with no errors.

As you work these addition problems, aim for accuracy rather than speed. Remember that even if a problem looks long, you still only need to add two numbers at a time!

■ Add.

1.2    3 + 4 = _____

1.3    13 + 4 = _____

1.4    23 + 4 = _____

1.5    33 + 4 = _____

1.6    8 + 2 = _____

1.7    18 + 2 = _____

1.8    28 + 2 = _____

1.9    58 + 2 = _____

1.10   9 + 3 = _____

1.11   19 + 3 = _____

1.12   29 + 3 = _____

1.13   79 + 3 = _____

1.14   5 + 6 = _____

1.15   15 + 6 = _____

1.16   25 + 6 = _____

1.17   45 + 6 = _____

1.18   75 + 5 = _____

1.19   75 + 6 = _____

1.20   75 + 7 = _____

1.21   75 + 8 = _____

1.22   87 + 3 = _____

1.23   87 + 4 = _____

1.24   87 + 5 = _____

1.25   87 + 6 = _____

1.26   95 + 5 = _____

1.27   95 + 6 = _____

1.28   95 + 7 = _____

1.29   95 + 8 = _____

1.30   98 + 2 = _____

1.31   98 + 3 = _____

1.32   98 + 4 = _____

1.33   98 + 5 = _____

You may want to check your answers before you move on to the rest of the addition problems.

**Add.**

1.34   7 + 6 = _____          1.42   14 + 7 = _____

1.35   6 + 9 = _____          1.43    9 + 8 = _____

1.36   3 + 9 = _____          1.44   17 + 6 = _____

1.37   6 + 8 = _____          1.45   19 + 7 = _____

1.38   3 + 6 = _____          1.46   19 + 5 = _____

1.39  13 + 4 = _____          1.47   21 + 6 = _____

1.40  15 + 4 = _____          1.48   17 + 5 = _____

1.41  12 + 7 = _____

1.49   7 + 6 + 4 + 6 + 8 = _____

1.50   6 + 9 + 4 + 7 + 3 = _____

1.51   3 + 9 + 7 + 5 + 8 = _____

1.52   6 + 8 + 7 + 6 + 5 = _____

1.53   3 + 6 + 8 + 5 + 7 = _____

1.54  27 + 6 + 8 + 9 + 5 = _____

1.55  35 + 4 + 8 + 3 + 9 = _____

1.56  69 + 7 + 5 + 4 + 8 = _____

1.57  39 + 8 + 7 + 3 + 5 = _____

| 1.58 | 1.59 | 1.60 | 1.61 | 1.62 |
|------|------|------|------|------|
| 7    | 9    | 3    | 9    | 3    |
| 6    | 8    | 7    | 9    | 8    |
| 3    | 5    | 6    | 7    | 5    |
| 2    | 4    | 8    | 6    | 7    |
| + 5  | + 3  | + 9  | + 2  | + 6  |

| 1.63 | 1.64 | 1.65 |
|------|------|------|
| 9    | 6    | 7    |
| 3    | 2    | 5    |
| 5    | 9    | 9    |
| 4    | 7    | 6    |
| + 7  | + 8  | + 4  |

| | | | | |
|---|---|---|---|---|
| 1.66   68<br>   + 21 | 1.67   54<br>   + 25 | 1.68   63<br>   + 24 | 1.69   36<br>   + 26 | 1.70   78<br>   + 24 |
| 1.71   89<br>   + 16 | 1.72   67<br>   + 22 | 1.73   38<br>   + 49 | 1.74   47<br>   + 28 | 1.75   33<br>   + 42 |
| 1.76   94<br>   + 87 | 1.77   69<br>   + 67 | 1.78   43<br>   + 28 | 1.79   71<br>   + 19 | 1.80   36<br>   + 89 |
| 1.81   48<br>   + 29 | 1.82   73<br>   + 27 | 1.83   83<br>   + 29 | 1.84   787<br>   + 7 | 1.85   634<br>   + 9 |
| 1.86   257<br>   + 8 | 1.87   306<br>   + 6 | 1.88   289<br>   + 4 | 1.89   794<br>   + 50 | 1.90   643<br>   + 60 |
| 1.91   265<br>   + 40 | 1.92   312<br>   + 90 | 1.93   293<br>   + 70 | 1.94   844<br>   + 600 | 1.95   703<br>   + 800 |
| 1.96   305<br>   + 400 | 1.97   402<br>   + 600 | 1.98   363<br>   + 500 | 1.99   787<br>   + 657 | 1.100   634<br>   + 869 |

## SUBTRACTION

You probably remember that subtraction is very much like reverse addition. If 2 + 3 = 5, then 5 - 3 = 2 and 5 - 2 = 3. A good knowledge of the basic addition facts will help you to work the subtraction exercises in this section.

**Subtract.**

| | | | | |
|---|---|---|---|---|
| 1.101 | 6 - 3 = _____ | | 1.115 | 41 - 6 = _____ |
| 1.102 | 16 - 3 = _____ | | 1.116 | 81 - 6 = _____ |
| 1.103 | 26 - 3 = _____ | | 1.117 | 25 - 5 = _____ |
| 1.104 | 36 - 3 = _____ | | 1.118 | 25 - 6 = _____ |
| 1.105 | 10 - 7 = _____ | | 1.119 | 25 - 7 = _____ |
| 1.106 | 20 - 7 = _____ | | 1.120 | 43 - 3 = _____ |
| 1.107 | 30 - 7 = _____ | | 1.121 | 43 - 4 = _____ |
| 1.108 | 60 - 7 = _____ | | 1.122 | 43 - 5 = _____ |
| 1.109 | 17 - 9 = _____ | | 1.123 | 76 - 6 = _____ |
| 1.110 | 27 - 9 = _____ | | 1.124 | 76 - 7 = _____ |
| 1.111 | 37 - 9 = _____ | | 1.125 | 76 - 8 = _____ |
| 1.112 | 57 - 9 = _____ | | 1.126 | 97 - 7 = _____ |
| 1.113 | 11 - 6 = _____ | | 1.127 | 97 - 8 = _____ |
| 1.114 | 21 - 6 = _____ | | 1.128 | 97 - 9 = _____ |

You may want to check your subtraction answers before proceeding.

**Subtract.**

| | | | | | | | | |
|---|---|---|---|---|---|---|---|---|
| 1.129 | 73<br>- 30 | 1.130 | 96<br>- 40 | 1.131 | 57<br>- 23 | 1.132 | 45<br>- 38 |

| | | | | | | | | |
|---|---|---|---|---|---|---|---|---|
| 1.133 | 51<br>- 32 | 1.134 | 73<br>- 32 | 1.135 | 96<br>- 46 | 1.136 | 48<br>- 17 |

| | | | | | | | | |
|---|---|---|---|---|---|---|---|---|
| 1.137 | 69<br>- 35 | 1.138 | 82<br>- 64 | 1.139 | 73<br>- 38 | 1.140 | 96<br>- 48 |

7

| | | | |
|---|---|---|---|
| 1.141 $\begin{array}{r} 78 \\ -29 \\ \hline \end{array}$ | 1.142 $\begin{array}{r} 94 \\ -27 \\ \hline \end{array}$ | 1.143 $\begin{array}{r} 49 \\ -38 \\ \hline \end{array}$ | 1.144 $\begin{array}{r} 541 \\ -8 \\ \hline \end{array}$ |
| 1.145 $\begin{array}{r} 541 \\ -28 \\ \hline \end{array}$ | 1.146 $\begin{array}{r} 807 \\ -60 \\ \hline \end{array}$ | 1.147 $\begin{array}{r} 732 \\ -28 \\ \hline \end{array}$ | 1.148 $\begin{array}{r} 823 \\ -15 \\ \hline \end{array}$ |
| 1.149 $\begin{array}{r} 541 \\ -20 \\ \hline \end{array}$ | 1.150 $\begin{array}{r} 807 \\ -9 \\ \hline \end{array}$ | 1.151 $\begin{array}{r} 807 \\ -69 \\ \hline \end{array}$ | 1.152 $\begin{array}{r} 465 \\ -59 \\ \hline \end{array}$ |
| 1.153 $\begin{array}{r} 396 \\ -77 \\ \hline \end{array}$ | 1.154 $\begin{array}{r} 530 \\ -120 \\ \hline \end{array}$ | 1.155 $\begin{array}{r} 457 \\ -283 \\ \hline \end{array}$ | 1.156 $\begin{array}{r} 642 \\ -176 \\ \hline \end{array}$ |
| 1.157 $\begin{array}{r} 423 \\ -378 \\ \hline \end{array}$ | 1.158 $\begin{array}{r} 710 \\ -296 \\ \hline \end{array}$ | 1.159 $\begin{array}{r} 906 \\ -557 \\ \hline \end{array}$ | 1.160 $\begin{array}{r} 726 \\ -314 \\ \hline \end{array}$ |
| 1.161 $\begin{array}{r} 806 \\ -572 \\ \hline \end{array}$ | 1.162 $\begin{array}{r} 507 \\ -169 \\ \hline \end{array}$ | 1.163 $\begin{array}{r} 584 \\ -387 \\ \hline \end{array}$ | 1.164 $\begin{array}{r} 600 \\ -432 \\ \hline \end{array}$ |
| 1.165 $\begin{array}{r} 213 \\ -159 \\ \hline \end{array}$ | 1.166 $\begin{array}{r} 5,679 \\ -3,908 \\ \hline \end{array}$ | 1.167 $\begin{array}{r} 4,619 \\ -1,837 \\ \hline \end{array}$ | 1.168 $\begin{array}{r} 3,706 \\ -1,829 \\ \hline \end{array}$ |
| 1.169 $\begin{array}{r} 6,001 \\ -2,095 \\ \hline \end{array}$ | 1.170 $\begin{array}{r} 83,296 \\ -17,259 \\ \hline \end{array}$ | 1.171 $\begin{array}{r} 4,821 \\ -2,096 \\ \hline \end{array}$ | 1.172 $\begin{array}{r} 7,295 \\ -6,489 \\ \hline \end{array}$ |
| 1.173 $\begin{array}{r} 5,037 \\ -2,976 \\ \hline \end{array}$ | 1.174 $\begin{array}{r} 3,000 \\ -1,234 \\ \hline \end{array}$ | 1.175 $\begin{array}{r} 40,076 \\ -21,087 \\ \hline \end{array}$ | |

Figure 2 is a table of the basic multiplication facts. To read the table, choose a number in the top row that you wish to multiply. Choose another number in the left-hand column you wish to multiply by the first number. Follow the column of the top number to its intersection with the left-hand number. The intersection shows the answer for multiplying the numbers together.

| X | 0 | 1 | 2 | 3 | 4 | 5 | 6 | 7 | 8 | 9 |
|---|---|---|---|---|---|---|---|---|---|---|
| 0 | 0 | 0 | 0 | 0 | 0 | 0 | 0 | 0 | 0 | 0 |
| 1 | 0 | 1 | 2 | 3 | 4 | 5 | 6 | 7 | 8 | 9 |
| 2 | 0 | 2 | 4 | 6 | 8 | 10 | 12 | 14 | 16 | 18 |
| 3 | 0 | 3 | 6 | 9 | 12 | 15 | 18 | 21 | 24 | 27 |
| 4 | 0 | 4 | 8 | 12 | 16 | 20 | 24 | 28 | 32 | 36 |
| 5 | 0 | 5 | 10 | 15 | 20 | 25 | 30 | 35 | 40 | 45 |
| 6 | 0 | 6 | 12 | 18 | 24 | 30 | 36 | 42 | 48 | 54 |
| 7 | 0 | 7 | 14 | 21 | 28 | 35 | 42 | 49 | 56 | 63 |
| 8 | 0 | 8 | 16 | 24 | 32 | 40 | 48 | 56 | 64 | 72 |
| 9 | 0 | 9 | 18 | 27 | 36 | 45 | 54 | 63 | 72 | 81 |

Figure 2

To check how well you know the multiplication facts, work on the following chart. Time yourself to see how quickly you do it. (If a stopwatch is available, use it.) Accuracy is more important than speed!

■ Complete this basic multiplication chart.

1.176

| X | 3 | 0 | 2 | 6 | 4 | 9 | 7 | 1 | 8 | 5 |
|---|---|---|---|---|---|---|---|---|---|---|
| 1 | | | | | | | | | | |
| 5 | | | | | | | | | | |
| 3 | | | | | | | | | | |
| 9 | | | | | | | | | | |
| 8 | | | | | | | | | | |
| 6 | | | | | | | | | | |
| 2 | | | | | | | | | | |
| 4 | | | | | | | | | | |
| 7 | | | | | | | | | | |
| 0 | | | | | | | | | | |

Time:  minutes  _____

seconds  _____

Number missed  _____

As you work these multiplication problems, remember that multiplication is actually repeated addition.  Your knowledge of the basic facts should be very useful to you in this section.

■ Multiply.

| 1.177 | 60<br>x 3 | 1.178 | 92<br>x 4 | 1.179 | 81<br>x 9 | 1.180 | 54<br>x 2 |
|---|---|---|---|---|---|---|---|

| 1.181 | 72<br>x 3 | 1.182 | 62<br>x 2 | 1.183 | 40<br>x 9 | 1.184 | 71<br>x 8 |
|---|---|---|---|---|---|---|---|

1.185    93     1.186    82     1.187    91     1.188    53
        x 3               x 4               x 7               x 2

1.189    16     1.190    54     1.191    23     1.192    35
        x 3               x 4               x 7               x 5

1.193    74     1.194    88
        x 9               x 8

Check your answers before you go on to the rest of the multiplication exercises.

**Multiply.**

1.195    63     1.196    73     1.197    95     1.198    62
        x 5               x 8               x 3               x 9

1.199    85     1.200    87     1.201    96     1.202    57
        x 4               x 8               x 4               x 4

1.203    49     1.204    58     1.205    34     1.206    24
        x 8               x 5               x 3               x 6

1.207    84     1.208    66     1.209    26     1.210    19
        x 9               x 6               x 3               x 6

1.211    48     1.212    39     1.213    369     1.214    783
        x 6               x 7               x 7               x 4

| | | | |
|---|---|---|---|
| 1.215    6,248 <br> x 6 | 1.216    9,284 <br> x 3 | 1.217    6,209 <br> x 4 | 1.218    628 <br> x 9 |
| 1.219    839 <br> x 5 | 1.220    3,719 <br> x 7 | 1.221    8,317 <br> x 8 | 1.222    7,036 <br> x 5 |
| 1.223    16 <br> x 20 | 1.224    54 <br> x 20 | 1.225    23 <br> x 40 | 1.226    35 <br> x 60 |
| 1.227    74 <br> x 10 | 1.228    88 <br> x 30 | 1.229    16 <br> x 23 | 1.230    54 <br> x 24 |
| 1.231    23 <br> x 47 | 1.232    35 <br> x 65 | 1.233    74 <br> x 19 | 1.234    88 <br> x 38 |
| 1.235    74 <br> x 39 | 1.236    58 <br> x 17 | 1.237    64 <br> x 27 | 1.238    68 <br> x 91 |
| 1.239    81 <br> x 42 | 1.240    75 <br> x 23 | 1.241    38 <br> x 45 | 1.242    39 <br> x 25 |
| 1.243    36 <br> x 28 | 1.244    47 <br> x 26 | 1.245    76 <br> x 63 | 1.246    69 <br> x 56 |
| 1.247    486 <br> x 21 | 1.248    213 <br> x 165 | 1.249    198 <br> x 751 | 1.250    872 <br> x 534 |
| 1.251    7,204 <br> x 618 | 1.252    673 <br> x 46 | 1.253    109 <br> x 23 | 1.254    134 <br> x 649 |

| 1.255 | 451 | 1.256 | 3,192 |
|---|---|---|---|
| | x 107 | | x 823 |

∿∿∿∿∿∿∿∿∿∿ **DIVISION** ∿∿∿∿∿∿∿∿∿∿∿∿∿∿∿∿∿∿∿∿∿∿∿∿∿∿∿∿∿∿∿

In the same way that subtraction can be thought of as reverse addition, division can be looked upon as reverse multiplication. In fact, division is a review, all by itself, of your knowledge of the other basic facts!

Model 1:

```
        33 R1
    3 )100
         9
        10
         9
         1
```

Model 2:

```
       189 R3
    4 )759
        4
        35
        32
        39
        36
         3
```

Do your best on these division exercises. Remember to work for accuracy rather than speed.

**Divide.**

| 1.257 | 6 )26 | 1.258 | 5 )32 | 1.259 | 9 )40 |
|---|---|---|---|---|---|

1.260  6 )41    1.261  8 )66    1.262  7 )31

1.263  3 )28    1.264  8 )27    1.265  7 )38

1.266  9 )80

Check your division answers before you do
the rest of the exercises in this section.

██████  Divide.

1.267  3 )748    1.268  4 )827    1.269  5 )604

1.270  7 )938    1.271  8 )357    1.272  6 )768

1.273  8 )940    1.274  2 )117    1.275  5 )491

1.276  9 )839    1.277  3 )472    1.278  6 )479

1.279  8 )789    1.280  4 )834    1.281  6 )727

14

1.282  3 )287⎺      1.283  4 )267⎺      1.284  7 )680⎺

1.285  9 )872⎺      1.286  4 )934⎺      1.287  5 )624⎺

1.288  9 )586⎺      1.289  3 )238⎺      1.290  3 )791⎺

1.291  7 )998⎺      1.292  4 )657⎺      1.293  8 )947⎺

1.294  3 )706⎺      1.295  7 )947⎺      1.296  6 )827⎺

1.297  7 )709⎺      1.298  5 )473⎺      1.299  4 )425⎺

1.300  9 )974⎺      1.301  9 )570⎺      1.302  3 )743⎺

1.303  4 )327⎺      1.304  5 )684⎺      1.305  7 )914⎺

1.306  8 )658⎺      1.307  6 )769⎺      1.308  8 )941⎺

1.309    2 )417      1.310    5 )791      1.311    9 )726

        Are you still in doubt about any of the basic arithmetic facts?  Probably not!  Now you are ready to use these basic facts in creative and inventive ways in the next section of this LIFEPAC.

 Review the material in this section in preparation for the Self Test. The Self Test will check your mastery of this particular section. The items missed on this Self Test will indicate specific areas where restudy is needed for mastery.

## SELF TEST 1

Add (each answer, 3 points).

| 1.01 | 1.02 | 1.03 | 1.04 | 1.05 |
|------|------|------|------|------|
| 62 | 38 | 71 | 693 | 472 |
| 48 | 46 | 20 | 208 | 278 |
| 27 | 27 | 86 | 471 | 694 |
| 95 | 69 | 94 | 289 | 73 |
| 46 | 58 | 38 | 617 | 217 |

Subtract (each answer, 3 points).

| 1.06 | 1.07 | 1.08 | 1.09 | 1.010 |
|------|------|------|------|-------|
| 674 | 824 | 681 | 4,006 | 3,001 |
| 289 | 369 | 497 | 2,794 | 1,684 |

**Multiply (each answer, 3 points).**

1.011   37
         5

1.012   71
         6

1.013   64
        49

1.014  318
         9

1.015  574
        31

1.016  44
        7

1.017  23
        8

1.018  56
      82

1.019 746
       5

1.020 602
     145

1.021  28
       6

1.022 487
      6

1.023  57
      29

1.024  45
     72

1.025 809
     65

**Divide (each answer, 3 points).**

1.026  4 )398     1.027  44 )93    1.028  75 )375  1.029  24 )643

1.030  5 )536     1.031  13 )79    1.032  81 )518  1.033  19 )217

1.034  9 )374     1.035  32 )752

84 / 105

Score _____

Teacher check _____

                 Initial     Date

# II. MENTAL SEARCH SKILLS

5. To solve mathematical puzzles.
6. To name the factors of whole numbers.
7. To identify prime numbers.

Although the basic skills are important, mathematics does not need to be just carrying out a technique that someone has shown us. Mathematics, if it is real and useful, involves creativity and discovery.

The purpose of this section is to help loosen up your feelings about mathematics. Learn to relax when you do mathematics, and use your imagination.

## PUZZLES

Much of mathematical thinking is like puzzle solving. Try to think creatively as you learn to solve these puzzles.

Model: *M* is a three-digit number.

Determine the digits of *M* from these clues.

All the digits are odd.
The last two digits add to make 4.
The first and last digits add to make 2.

Solution:

If the digits are odd, they must be either 1,3,5,7,or 9. If the last two digits add to make 4, they must be either 1 and 3 or 2 and 2. And since the digits must be odd, the last two digits must be 1 and 3. In what order do they go? The last clue will show us.

If the first and last digits add to make 2,
   they must be 1 and 1.  Therefore, the
   3 goes in the middle position.

M is 131.


■■■■  Solve these mathematical puzzles.


2.1  S is a three-digit number.

Determine the digits of S from these clues.

   All the digits are odd.
   The last two digits add to make ten.
   The first and last digits add to make eight.
   The first two digits add to make twelve.


2.2  Write two numbers that add to make twenty and have a difference
of four.

   _____   _____


2.3  Write two numbers that add to make 36 with one of the numbers
being exactly twice the other.

   _____


2.4  Across

   1.  361 plus 1,172
   2.  5 times the number in 3 Down

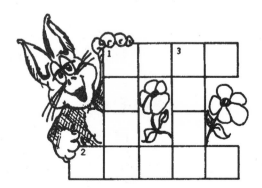

   Down

   1.  173 plus the number in 1 Across
   3.  The number in 1 Across plus the
       number in 1 Down

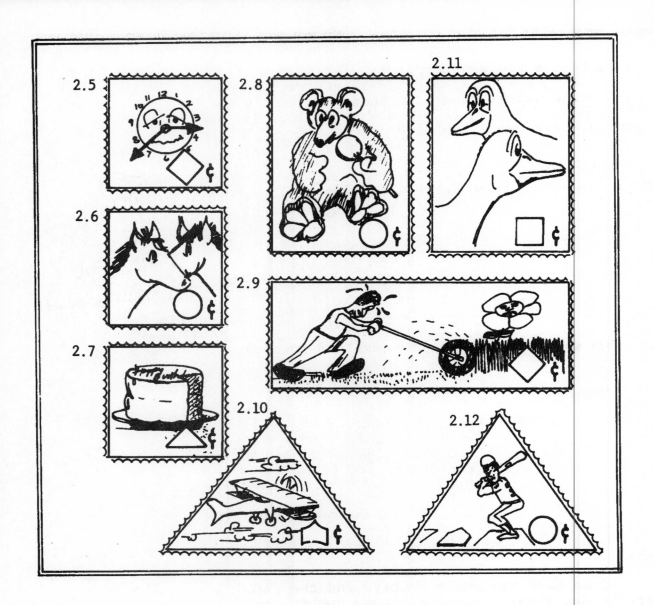

In this stamp collection, the value of each stamp is left blank.

Fill in the stamp values using the clues.

    The rectangle stamps total 24¢.
    The rectangle stamps with animals total 16¢.
    The triangle stamps altogether are worth 24¢.
    The square stamps total 11¢.
    The stamps with animals altogether are worth 20¢.
    The stamps with two animals are together worth 13¢.
    The two stamps with a person come to 22¢.
    The stamps with mechanical devices total 20¢.

What is a whole number?

A whole number is a certain number of 1's added together. Zero, which stands for no 1's, is also considered a whole number.

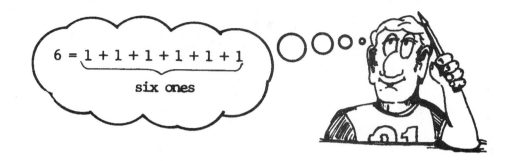

$$6 = \underbrace{1 + 1 + 1 + 1 + 1 + 1}_{\text{six ones}}$$

Two whole numbers can be combined in several ways.

They can be

ADDED,

SUBTRACTED,

MULTIPLIED, or

DIVIDED.

The tricky operation is division, because two whole numbers do not **always** divide evenly.

If we have two whole numbers and the first number divides evenly into the second number, then we say that the first number is a *factor* of the second number.

---

DEFINITION

*Factor*: a number that divides evenly into another number.

---

Write *true* or *false*.

2.13 _____ 2 is a factor of 6

2.14 _____ 6 is a factor of 2

2.15 _____ 3 is a factor of 12

2.16 _____ 1 is a factor of 1

2.17 _____ 5 is a factor of 12

2.18 _____ 12 is a factor of 6

2.19 _____ 12 is a factor of 24

2.20 _____ 1 is a factor of 12

████ Write a number in each blank to make the statements true.

2.21 A number that divides evenly into 24 is _____.

2.22 A factor of 24 is _____.

2.23 A factor of 28 is _____.

2.24 A factor of 33 is _____.

2.25 A factor of 64 is _____.

2.26 Four is a factor of _____.

2.27 Fifteen is a factor of _____.

2.28 A factor of 77 is _____.

2.29 Two factors of 64 are a. _____ and b. _____.

2.30 Seven and nine are both factors of _____.

████ Write true or false.

2.31 _____ Two is a factor of every even number.

2.32 _____ One is a factor of every number.

2.33 _____ Three is a factor of every odd number.

2.34 _____ Seven is a factor of 7.

2.35 _____ Every number is a factor of itself.

2.36 _____ Three is a factor of 97.

2.37 _____ A number exists that has 4 as a factor but that does not have 2 as a factor.

2.38 _____ A number exists that has 2 as a factor but that does not have 4 as a factor.

2.39 _____ Every number has itself and 1 as a factor.

▇▇▇ Complete these activities.

2.40 List all of the numbers that are factors of 15.

a. _____ b. _____ c. _____ d. _____

2.41 List all of the numbers that are factors of 20.

a. _____ b. _____ c. _____ d. _____ e. _____ f. _____

⚬⚬⚬⚬⚬⚬⚬ PRIME NUMBERS ⚬⚬⚬⚬⚬⚬⚬⚬⚬⚬⚬⚬⚬⚬⚬⚬⚬⚬⚬⚬

Remember that *every* number has 1 as a factor and also has itself as a factor. Some numbers have *only* 1 and itself as factors. A number that has only itself and 1 as factors is called a *prime number*.

DEFINITION
*Prime number*: a number that has only itself and 1 as factors. The number 1 is not considered a prime number.

Model 1: Circle the two numbers that are prime numbers.

9, 10, ⑪, 12, ⑬

Model 2: Circle the three numbers that are prime numbers.

⑦, 15, 21, 22, ㉓, ⑤

**■** Complete these activities.

2.42    A number between 30 and 40 that has only 1 and itself as

factors is _____.

2.43    A prime number between 40 and 45 is _____.

2.44    A prime number between 45 and 50 is _____.

A *prime factor* of a number is a factor that
happens to be a prime number.

---

DEFINITION

*Prime factor*:  a factor that is also a prime number.

---

Model 3:  Of the following factors of 24,
circle all of the prime factors.

1, ②, ③, 4, 6, 8, 12, 24

**■** Complete these activities.

2.45    Of the following factors of 28, circle all of the prime factors.

1, 2, 4, 7, 14, 28

2.46    List all of the prime factors of 20.

a. _____  b. _____

2.47    List all of the prime factors of 30.

a. _____  b. _____  c. _____

24

# CONSUMER MATHEMATICS 1

# LIFEPAC TEST

**Name** _____

**Date** _____

**Score** _____

# CONSUMER MATHEMATICS 1: LIFEPAC TEST

Write a number on each blank to make the statements true (each answer, 3 points).

1.  When a certain valve is open 281 gallons go through it in one hour.

    The number of gallons that would go through in 94 hours is

    _____ gallons.

2.  The barrels weighed 834 pounds apiece.

    The ship's cargo included 618 barrels.

    Therefore, the barrels added _____ pounds in weight to

    the ship's cargo.

3.
```
      __ 9
  x   __ 6
  _____
    1  1 __
    __  6
  _____
    __ __ 4
```

4.
```
      __ 4
  x   __ 3
  _____
    1  0 __
    __  8
  _____
    __ __ 2
```

5.
```
             __ __    R 1
        7) _____
             __ __
        2  1
        2  9
        2  8
        _____
```

6.  The largest prime factor of fifty-six is _____.

7.  The largest prime factor of thirty-four is _____.

8.    Each table has exactly five plates on it.

      Each plate has exactly seven radishes on it.

      You have twenty-one tables altogether.

      You have _____ radishes altogether.

9.    Each hour the train got closer to Kansas City.

      In the first hour it traveled 54 miles.

      In the first three hours it traveled 209 miles.

      In the third hour it traveled 82 miles.

      Therefore, during the second hour it must have traveled

      _____ miles.

10.   Each cabin had exactly 8 occupants.

      There were _____ cabins altogether.

      The number of occupants for all of the cabins was 208.

11.   Every page of the book had exactly 24 lines of print on it.

      The entire book had 10,224 lines of print in it.

      The book had _____ pages altogether.

# NOTES

2.48    The largest prime factor of 20 is _____ .

2.49    The largest prime factor of 28 is _____ .

2.50    The largest prime factor of 24 is _____ .

2.51    The largest prime factor of 7 is _____ .

2.52    The largest prime factor of 33 is _____ .

2.53    The largest prime factor of 34 is _____ .

2.54    The largest prime factor of 32 is _____ .

---

  Review the material in this section in preparation for the Self Test. This Self Test will check your mastery of this particular section as well as your knowledge of the previous section.

## SELF TEST 2

Solve these mathematical puzzles (each digit, 3 points).

2.01    R is a three-digit number.

Determine the digits of R from these clues.

        The first digit is the answer when the third digit is
            divided by 5.
        The second and third digits add to 8.
        The difference of the first and second digits is 2.

25

**2.02**   *Y* is a three-digit number.

**Determine** the digits of *Y* from these clues.

The digits of *Y* add to 16.
The first digit is 4 times the third digit.
The second digit is 3 times the third digit.

**2.03**   *Q* is a four-digit number.

**Determine** the digits of *Q* from these clues.

The first and third digits of *Q* are odd.
The second and fourth digits of *Q* are even.
The fourth digit is two times the first digit.
The first and second digits add to seven.
The second and third digits add to nine.
The third and fourth digits add to eleven.

**2.04**   *F* is a four-digit number.

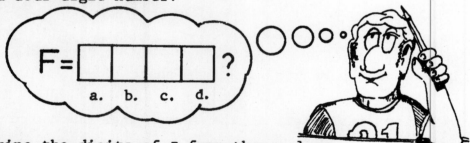

**Determine** the digits of *F* from these clues.

The digits of *F* are all the same.
The sum of all the digits of *F* is 16.
The answer when any two of the digits are multiplied
   together is also 16.

2.05   z is a four-digit number.

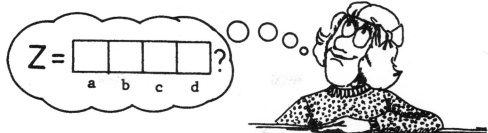

Determine the digits of z from these clues.

The first digit of z is the largest prime factor of 35.

The third digit of z is the smallest prime factor of 24, other than 1.

The last digit of z plus the first digit of z add to 12.

The second digit of z is the second largest prime factor of 110.

44 / 54

Score _____

Teacher check _____
Initial      Date

27

<table>
<tr>
<td>

### III. CREATIVE MANIPULATION SKILLS

</td>
<td>

**OBJECTIVE**

8.  To use creatively the basic skills of addition, subtraction, multiplication, and division.

</td>
</tr>
</table>

The purpose of this section is to have you adding, subtracting, multiplying, and dividing with ease.

**━━━━━ ADDITION AND SUBTRACTION ━━━━━**

These creative exercises use addition and subtraction. Have fun as you solve them!

**████** Write a number on each blank to make the statements true.

3.1 Hazel traveled 796 meters by foot, 3,486 meters by car, and 56,975 meters by hot air balloon. Hazel traveled _____ meters altogether.

3.2
```
  __ 6 __
+  2 __ 9
_____
   6  5  3
```

3.3
```
  __ 8  4
+  3 __ __
_____
   5  3  2
```

3.4
```
  __ 1  2
   4  3 __
+  5  5  1
_____
 __ 2 __ 4
```

**████** In the diagram:

3.5 The distance from A to F is _____ meters.

3.6 The distance from F to G is _____ meters.

3.7 The distance from H to G is _____ meters.

28

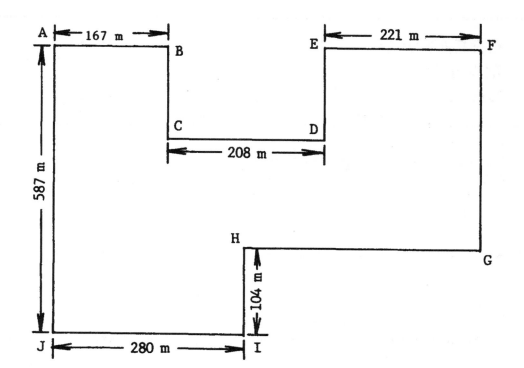

3.8
```
  7 __ __
-__  4  3
─────────
  3  2  1
```

3.9
```
  8  2 __
-__  6  4
─────────
  2 __  5
```

3.10
```
  __  1  3
   4  6  2
   3  8 __
+  2 __  6
──────────
__  3  5  2
```

3.11
```
  8  7 __
-__  8  2
─────────
  4 __  5
```

3.12
```
  6 __ __ __
- 2  8  7  3
────────────
__  2  4  5
```

3.13    Flora weighs 186 pounds.

Flora has lost _____ pounds since last year.

Last year Flora weighed 234 pounds.

3.14    When full, the truck holds _____ liters of gas in its tank.

Since the last fill-up the truck has used 39 liters of gas.

The truck now has 57 liters of gas in its tank.

3.15 Jethro received some profit this month from each one of his three stores.

From his shoe store, the profit was $438.

From his produce store, the profit was $938.

The profit from his convenience mart was _____.

From the three stores altogether he received $3,468.

3.16
```
    6  8  __
  + 2  __  9
  _____
     __  6  3
```

3.17
```
     2  __  7  6
   + 5  4  __  __
   _____
      __  3  6  7
```

3.18
```
     2  __  3  9
       __  4  __  6
   + 9  3  4  __
   _____
      __  9  9  6  2
```

3.19
```
     __  7  7
   -  6  __  __
   _____
      2  2  9
```

3.20
```
     __  5  4  2
   -  4  6  __  __
   _____
      1  __  8  4
```

3.21
```
     7  2  __  4
   -  __  8  3  __
   _____
      1  __  2  7
```

~~~~~~~~~~ MULTIPLICATION ~~~~~~~~~~

Multiplication is the key to solving this set of exercises. Remember to think creatively but also carefully. When you have decided what number is missing, then decide what numbers will multiply to give you the answer. If the answer is given, then decide the number you need for the answer to be correct.

Model: Write a number on each blank to make the statement true.

```
      1  5
    __  5
    _____
      7  __
  1  5  __
  _____
    __  2  5
```

In this model, you can see that the first blank should have 1 in it, because the matching product, 15, is 15 x 1. The second blank should have 5 in it, because 5 x 5 is 25. The third blank needs a 2, because 1 + 1 (carried from 7 + 5 = 12) is 2.

30

Write a number on each blank to make the statements true.

3.22
```
    __ 9
  x __ 6
  _____
    1 1 __
    __ 6
  _____
  __ __ 4
```

3.23
```
    __ 4
  x __ 3
  _____
    1 0 __
    __ 8
  _____
  __ __ 2
```

3.24
```
    2 __
  x __ 6
  _____
    1 4 __
    __ 2
  _____
    8 __ 4
```

3.25    When a certain valve is open, 57 gallons go through it in one hour.

Therefore, in two hours a. _____ gallons would go through.

In three hours b. _____ gallons would pass through.

Seven hours would be sufficient time for c. _____ gallons to pass through the valve.

3.26    The tire on a bicycle is 52 inches around.

When the bicycle is going forward in a straight line, every time the tire goes around the bicycle moves ahead exactly

a. _____ inches.

If the tire goes around two times, the bike will move ahead

b. _____ inches.

If the tire goes around 12 times, the bike will move ahead

c. _____ inches.

If the tire goes around 27 times, the bike will move ahead

d. _____ inches.

31

If the tire goes around 146 times, the bike will move ahead

e. _____ inches

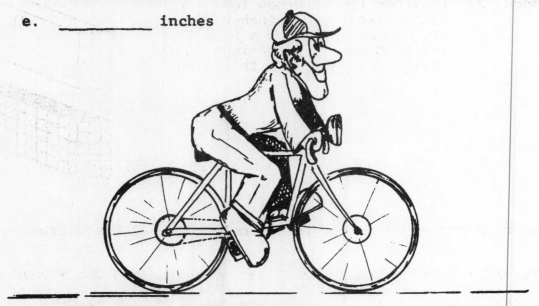

3.27    The pipe weighs 17 pounds per foot.

The pipe is 8 feet long.

Therefore, the pipe weighs _____ pounds altogether.

You may already be familiar with the concept of *volume*, which is measured in cubic units. Volume is a measure of the space "inside" a geometric figure and is found by multiplying the figure's length times its width times its height.

---

DEFINITION

*Volume*: length x width x height.

---

Model 1:    This cube is 10 inches long, 10 inches wide, and 10 inches high. Its volume is 10 x 10 x 10 or 1,000 cubic inches. You could say that 1,000 one-inch cubes could fit into a box this size.

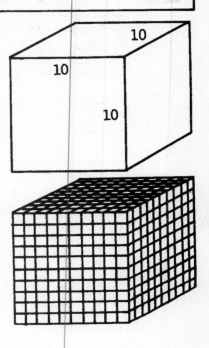

Model 2: This box is 11 inches long, 3 inches wide, and 5 inches high. Its volume is 11 x 3 x 5 or 165 cubic inches; 165 one-inch cubes could fit into a box this size.

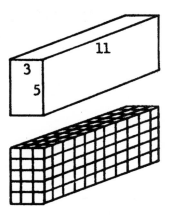

███████  Write a number on each blank to make the statements true.

3.28    The number of one-inch cubes that will fit into a box that is 6 inches wide, 9 inches long, and one inch high is _____.

3.29    The number of one-inch cubes that will fit into a box that is 9 inches wide, 13 inches long, and one inch high is _____.

3.30    The number of one-inch cubes that will fit into a box that is one inch wide, 20 inches long, and 14 inches high is _____.

3.31    The number of one-inch cubes that will fit into a box that is 2 inches wide, 20 inches long, and 14 inches high is _____.

███████  Complete the chart.

|  | Number of one-inch cubes that fit | Box Width (inches) | Box Length (inches) | Box Height (inches) |
|---|---|---|---|---|
| 3.32 |  | 2 | 17 | 1 |
| 3.33 |  | 2 | 17 | 2 |
| 3.34 |  | 2 | 17 | 3 |
| 3.35 |  | 2 | 17 | 9 |
| 3.36 |  | 8 | 7 | 1 |
| 3.37 |  | 8 | 7 | 3 |
| 3.38 |  | 1 | 14 | 15 |

| | Number of one-inch cubes that fit | Box Width (inches) | Box Length (inches) | Box Height (inches) |
|---|---|---|---|---|
| 3.39 | | 2 | 14 | 15 |
| 3.40 | | 9 | 14 | 15 |

3.41
```
      3 7
  x __ __
  _____
    3 3 3
    7 4
  _____
  __ __ __ __
```

3.42
```
      __ __ 4
  x __ __
  _____
  1 2 4 2
  8 2 8
  _____
  __ __ __ __
```

3.43
```
        __ __
  x   2  8
  _____
    2 7 2
  __ __
  _____
  __ __ __ __
```

3.44   When a certain valve is open, 281 gallons go through it in one hour.

The number of gallons that would go through in 91 hours is

_____ gallons.

3.45   The barrels weighed 834 pounds apiece.

The ship's cargo included 612 barrels.

Therefore, the barrels added _____ pounds in weight to the ship's cargo.

~~~~~~~~~ DIVISION ~~~~~~~~~

The next set of problems require you to use division to find the answer. Some exercises toward the end of the section also help review addition, subtraction, and multiplication.

34

Write a number on each blank to make the statements true.

3.46    Q is a three-digit number.

Determine the digits of Q from these clues.

    All the digits are odd.

    The number Q is evenly divisible by 15.

    The first two digits add to 10.

    No two digits are alike.

    The first digit is smaller than any of the other digits.

    The second and third digits add to 14.

3.47
```
        3 __    R __
     7 ) 2 __ 9
       __ __
         3 __
         3 __
           4
```

3.48
```
         __ __    R __
     9 ) 6 __ 4
       6 3
       4 __
       3 6
       __
```

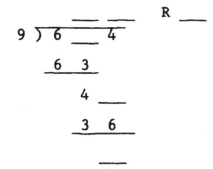

3.49    The tank contains 896 gallons of water.  The water must be
        shared equally among 112 persons.  Each person should receive
        _____ gallons of water.

**3.50**

```
                __  8  4   R 26
    27 )  __  __  9  4
          2  7  __
          2  2  __
             __  __  6
             __  __
                1  3  __
                1  0  8
                   __  __
```

**3.51**   Karen has a bag containing 423 rubber ducks.

If Karen gives 30 rubber ducks to each person she meets,
then she will have enough for a. _____ people; and
she will have b. _____ extra ducks left over.

**3.52**   John has a bag of 267 silver dollars.

If John gives five silver dollars to each person he meets,
then he will have enough for a. _____ people; and he
will have b. _____ extra silver dollars left over.

**3.53**

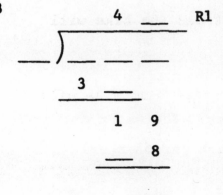

**3.54**

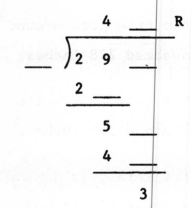

36

3.55

```
          __  2  R1
     __ ) 4  __  __
          4  8
             1  __
             1  2
                1
```

3.56

```
               1   7  __  R __ __
     __  __ ) 6   7  __  __
               __  9
               2  __  __
               __  __  __
               1   3  __
               1  __  __
                      __  5
```

3.57  The tire on a bicycle is 52 inches around.

When the bicycle is moving in a straight line, every time the tire goes around the bicycle moves forward exactly a. _____ inches.

If the tire goes around b. _____ times, the bike will move ahead 104 inches.

If the tire goes around c. _____ times the bike will move ahead 208 inches.

If the tire goes around d. _____ times, the bike will move ahead 364 inches.

If the tire goes around e. _____ times, the bike will move ahead 624 inches.

If the tire goes around f. _____ times, the bike will move ahead 1,976 inches.

37

The exercises from now on might use addition, subtraction, multiplication, or division. Your task, to determine which operation is needed, and then to solve the problem, should be easy and fun.

███ Write a number on each blank to make the statements true.

3.58
```
  6, 2 0 __
  __, __ 6 3
+ 7, 3 __ 9
_____
  __ 8, 1 1 4
```

3.59
```
  2, __ 6 1
  4, 9 __ 2
+ __, 4 7 __
_____
  __ 6, 7 1 7
```

3.60 If $3,978 is to be shared equally among 17 persons, then each

person should get exactly $_____.

3.61 The garden had 1,233 bees.

The garden also had 137 flowers.

Each of the bees was on one of the flowers.

Each flower had the same number of bees as the others.

Therefore, each flower had exactly _____ bees on it.

3.62 The company had 37 repairmen to take service orders.

One day 1,036 service orders were received.

If each repairman took the same number of orders as

the others, then each repairman took _____ orders.

3.63 The number of one-inch cubes that will fit into a box that is

6 inches wide, _____ inches long, and one inch tall is 54.

3.64 The number of one-inch cubes that will fit into a box that is

7 inches wide, _____ inches long, and one inch high is 154.

3.65 The number of one-inch cubes that will fit into a box that is 9 inches wide, 14 inches long, and one inch high is _____.

3.66 The number of one-inch cubes that will fit into a box that is _____ inches wide, 17 inches long, and one inch high is 102.

3.67
```
    __ 1  7
     3  6 __
     2  9  8
  +  8 __  7
  -----------
  __  7  2  3
```

3.68
```
          __  6  R6
    __ ) __  6 __
          4 __
          ------
          4 __
          4 __
          ------
          __
```

3.69
```
     6  4  7
    __  5  6
     9  2  5
  +  7 __ __
  -----------
  __  2  1  7
```

3.70 The cost of the item was $87 per case. The cost of an entire shipment of _____ cases was $1,218.

3.71 George was paid $6 per hour for his work.

He worked _____ hours.

George received $78 for his work.

3.72 On Mr. Jones' farm were exactly 6 cows for every pig.

Mr. Jones had _____ pigs.

He had 114 cows.

3.73 The cost of the paint was $39 per gallon, so the cost for a shipment of _____ gallons would be $4,368.

Is your mind as good as you want it to be?
You can improve your mind.  Simply by wishing to,
and by putting energy into your own mental growth,
you can realize an expansion of your capabilities.

Most of us tend to accept the idea that we
are born with certain limits.  We *can* grow, however;
this section of the LIFEPAC is specifically designed
to help you develop some of those mental capabilities.
You will find that the exercises in this section
require you to think a great deal, and many times to
picture clearly what you are thinking about.  Here's
to your mental growth!

## INDIVIDUAL ACTIVITIES

These exercises, which you can do alone, will
serve as a warm-up for the shared activities.
Feel your mental muscles stretch!

███  Write a number on each blank to make the statements true.

3.74    Each box has four jars in it.

You have six boxes altogether.

Each jar has four eggs in it.

You have a. _____ jars and b. _____ eggs altogether.

3.75    Each paper clip can be traded for three matches.

Each pencil can be traded for six paper clips.

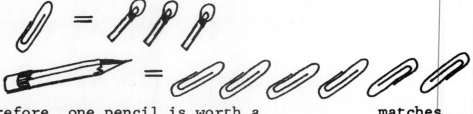

Therefore, one pencil is worth a. _____ matches.

Five paper clips are worth b. _____ matches.

Three pencils and four paper clips together are equal in

value to c. _____ matches.

Two pencils and nine matches together are equal in value

to d. _____ paper clips.

■■■■ Write *more than*, *less than*, or *equal to* to make the statements true. Refer to Problem 3.75.

3.76 Twelve matches are worth _____ two pencils and one paper clip.

3.77 Three pencils are worth _____ seventeen paper clips.

3.78 Two pencils and two paper clips are worth _____ thirty-eight matches.

3.79 Twenty-two paper clips are worth _____ sixty-seven matches.

3.80 Five pencils and two matches are worth _____ thirty paper clips.

■■■■ Mental Arithmetic: work the following exercises in your head. Do not calculate with a pencil or paper.

3.81 Think of the number seven.
Now add eight to it.
Now add four more.
Now subtract nine.

Write your answer: _____

3.82 Think of the number forty-seven.
Subtract nine from it.
Now add six.
Now subtract eight.
Now add three.
Now subtract seven.

Write your answer: _____

3.83 Think of the number eleven.
Now add seven to it.
Now subtract nine.
Now add six.
Now subtract four.
Now add nine.

Your answer: _____

3.84 Think of the number twenty-eight.
Add thirty-one to it.

Write your answer: _____

3.85 Think of the number forty-six.
Add twelve to it.
Now add eight.

Write your answer: _____

3.86 Think of the number thirty-two.
Subtract five from it.
Now add seven.
Now add eight.
Now subtract six.

Write your answer: _____

41

3.87     Think of the number
fifty-three.
Add twenty-five to it.
Now subtract nine.

Write your answer: _____

■■■■■    Write a number on each blank to make the statements true.

3.88     The price of one necklace is the same as the price of five

rings.  One ring costs $320.  The cost of a necklace is $_____.

3.89     The cost of two motorcycles is the same as the cost of seven

bicycles.  The cost of one bicycle is $152.  Therefore, the

cost of one motorcycle is $_____.

3.90     Every employee works 7 hours per day.

Every employee works 5 days per week.

Every employee works 49 weeks per year.

Every employee works a. _____ days per year.

Every employee works b. _____ hours per year.

3.91     One red chip is equal in value to four white chips.

One blue chip is equal in value to seven white chips.

Therefore, two red chips and one blue chip would be equal

in value to a. _____ white chips.

Also, three red chips and two blue chips would be equal in

value to b. _____ white chips.

3.92    One orange chip is equal in value to six white chips.

One purple chip is equal in value to two orange chips.

One purple chip is equal to a. _____ white chips.

Three purple chips equal b. _____ white chips.

Twenty-four white chips are equal to c. _____ orange chips.

Thirty-eight orange chips are equal to d. _____ purple chips.

3.93    A typist types five letters every hour.

Each typist works seven hours per day.

Three typists are working in the office.

Therefore, _____ letters can be typed each day in the office.


## SHARED ACTIVITIES

The following mental imagery activities require more than one person.  Try to make a new friend as you enjoy the activities.

MENTAL TIC-TAC-TOE.  This activity needs three people.  Choose two other people in your class to work with, preferably people you normally don't talk to often.

Make a chart such as the one shown below.  One person is the Chartkeeper, one person is X, and one person is O.

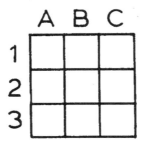

The Chartkeeper does not let the others see the chart.  X goes first by calling out the letter and number of the square he wants to take; O's turn works the same way.  The Chartkeeper records these moves. If a player calls out the letter and number of a square already occupied, then he loses his turn.  The first person to get three in a row, as in ordinary tic-tac-toe, is the winner.  For more advanced play use a four-by-four chart and require *four* in a row to win.

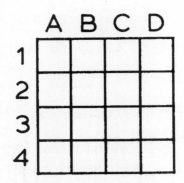

A B C D

1
2
3
4

MENTAL QUICKNESS DRILL.  This activity requires two people.  One person acts as the Caller, and one is the Responder.  The Caller takes this list and circles any three of the five colors in each row.

1)  RED    BLUE    YELLOW    GREEN    BLACK

2)  RED    GREEN    BLACK    YELLOW    BLUE

3)  GREEN    YELLOW    BLACK    BLUE    RED

4)  BLACK    GREEN    YELLOW    RED    BLUE

5)  GREEN    BLACK    BLUE    YELLOW    RED

6)  YELLOW    BLACK    BLUE    RED    GREEN

7)  GREEN    RED    BLUE    BLACK    YELLOW

8)  YELLOW    RED    GREEN    BLUE    BLACK

9)  BLACK    BLUE    YELLOW    RED    GREEN

10)  BLUE    GREEN    RED    YELLOW    BLACK

Holding the list so the Responder cannot see, the Caller calls out the circled items on the list, using one row at a time.  The Responder then calls back the two colors that the Caller left out. The Caller should put an 'X' on the choices the Responder gives to keep a record.

The Caller should use a watch with a sweep hand and start a new row every three to six seconds, determined at the beginning by the degree of challenge the Responder wants to take.

Good advice, when you are the Responder, is to go by the first impression that hits you.  Taking extra time to be *sure* (by picturing in your mind or some other technique) is foolish.  Going by your first impression leads to errors at first, but your perception will straighten itself out and soon you will be responding quickly and very accurately.

For more challenge play the game with digits instead of colors, replacing red with 1, blue with 2, yellow with 3, green with 4, and black with 5.

For even more challenge use six digits instead of five.

REVIEW

**Before** you take this last Self Test, you may want to do one or more of these self checks.

1. _____ Read the objectives. Determine if you can do them.

2. _____ Restudy the material related to any objectives that you cannot do

3. _____ Use the SQ3R study procedure to review the material:
   a. **S**can the sections.
   b. **Q**uestion yourself again (review the questions you wrote initially).
   c. **R**ead to answer your questions.
   d. **R**ecite the answers to yourself.
   e. **R**eview areas you didn't understand.

4. _____ Review all activities and Self Tests, writing a correct answer for each wrong answer.

## SELF TEST 3

Write a number in each blank to make the statements true (each answer, 3 points).

3.01    Each box has nine jars in it.

You have seven boxes altogether.

Each jar has two eggs in it.

Each egg has two baby dinosaurs in it.

You have a. _____ jars and b. _____ baby dinosaurs altogether.

3.02    Each month the stock decreased in value.

On January 1 it was worth $8,474.

On March 1 it was worth $3,323.

During February it decreased by $1,621.

During January it decreased by $ _____.

45

3.03    Flora weighs 186 pounds.

Flora has lost _____ pounds since last year.

Last year Flora weighed 234 pounds.


3.04
```
              __ 8 __ R 1 __
      17 ) __ , __ __ __
           3  4
           1  4  __
          _____
              __ __ __
              1  3  __
              1  1  9
             _____
                 __ 6
```

3.05
```
           __ 8  3
      x       __ __
      _____
      1, 2  8  1
        __  6  6
      _____
      __ , __ __ __
```


Information:

3.06    Each Indian is riding on a pony with exactly one other Indian.

Each pony has exactly two Indians on it.

Each pony has exactly three water bottles on him.

Twenty-two Indians altogether are riding.

They have _____ water bottles altogether.

3.07    Every employee works 9 hours per day.

Every employee works 5 days per week.

Every employee works 47 weeks per year.

Every employee works a. _____ days per year.

Every employee works b. _____ hours per year.

3.08    In the orchard were _____ apple trees.

Each tree in the orchard had exactly 118 apples on it.

The number of apples in the whole orchard was 2,242.

3.09    The bookcase had _____ books in it.

The bookcase had nine shelves.

Each shelf had exactly 23 books on it.

3.010   Six pencils are equal in value to two rulers.

One ruler is equal in value to two erasers.

Twelve pencils are equal in value to a. _____ erasers.

Two erasers are equal in value to b. _____ pencils.

One ruler and four erasers equal the value of c. _____
pencils.

3.011   The largest prime factor of thirty-five is _____.

3.012   The largest prime factor of thirty-eight is _____.

3.013   The second largest prime factor of thirty-eight is _____.

3.014   The smallest prime factor of twelve is _____.

3.015   The largest prime factor of twelve is _____.

92/114

Score _____
Teacher check _____
Initial        Date

**Before taking the LIFEPAC Test, you may want to do one or more of these self checks.**

1. _____ Read the objectives. Check to see if you can do them.
2. _____ Restudy the material related to any objective that you cannot do.
3. _____ Use the SQ3R study procedure to review the material.
4. _____ Review activities, Self Tests, and LIFEPAC Glossary.
5. _____ Restudy areas of weakness indicated by the last Self Test.

# GLOSSARY

*factor.* A number that divides evenly into another number.

*prime factor.* A factor that is also a prime number.

*prime number.* A number that has only itself and 1 as factors.

*volume.* A measure of the space within a geometric figure; length x width x height.